AI MASTERY SOLUTIONS

Mastering ChatGPT: Advanced Techniques for Generating Text with OpenAI

AI Mastery
Solutions

This book was professionally typeset on Reedsy.
Find out more at reedsy.com

This book is dedicated to all the computer programmers, data scientists, AI enthusiasts, and anyone else who is passionate about harnessing the power of advanced language models to generate text. Your curiosity and drive to learn and innovate is what makes this field so exciting and dynamic. May this book be a valuable resource on your journey to mastering ChatGPT and other AI technologies.

Contents

1

Chapter 1: Setting up ChatGPT

ChatGPT is a powerful language model developed by OpenAI that can generate a wide range of text, from simple responses to complex stories and articles. To fully utilize the capabilities of ChatGPT, you'll need to install the OpenAI API and any necessary extensions on your computer. This chapter will provide a step-by-step guide for setting up ChatGPT and getting started with using the API.

Step 1: Install the OpenAI API The first step in setting up ChatGPT is to install the OpenAI API. You can do this by going to the OpenAI website (**https://openai.com/**) and clicking on the "Get API Key" button on the top right corner of the page.

You will be prompted to create an account or sign in with an existing account. Once you have an account, you can generate an API key, which you will use to make calls to the API and access the capabilities of ChatGPT. Keep the API key safe, as it is used to track usage and bill your account.

Step 2: Install a Programming Language To use the OpenAI API, you'll need to install a programming language such as Python, JavaScript or any other language that has an SDK that can be used to call the API. If you're new to programming, Python is a great choice as it is easy to learn and has a large community that supports it.

To install Python, you can go to the official Python website (**https://www.python.org/downloads/**) and download the latest version of Python for your operating system. Once the download is complete, you can install it by following the on-screen instructions.

Step 3: Install Required Libraries After installing the programming language, you'll need to install the necessary libraries to interact with the OpenAI API. For Python, you can use the openai package which can be installed by running the command **pip install openai** in your command prompt or terminal.

To open the command prompt on windows press the windows key and type **cmd** and press enter, on MacOS and Linux the terminal can be opened by searching for it in the spotlight search or by pressing **ctrl+alt+T**

Step 4: Test the API connection Once you've completed all the above steps, you can test your API connection by running a simple script that makes a call to the API and returns the response. Here's an example of a simple Python script that uses the openai package to generate text using ChatGPT:

```python
import openai

# Use your API key to authenticate
openai.api_key = "YOUR_API_KEY"

# Define the prompt
prompt = "What is the capital of France?"

# Make the API call
response = openai.Completion.create(engine="text-davinci-002",
prompt=prompt)

# Print the response
print(response["choices"][0]["text"])
```

You can copy and paste the above script and replace **YOUR_API_KEY** with your own API key and run it on your machine. The script should return the capital of France which is "Paris".

Step 5: Install any additional extensions Depending on your specific use case, you may need to install additional extensions or libraries to fully utilize the capabilities of ChatGPT. For example, if you plan to use ChatGPT for natural language processing tasks, you may need to install NLTK or spaCy.

To install NLTK, you can run the command **pip install nltk** in your command prompt or terminal. Similarly, to install spaCy, you can run the command **pip install spacy**. Once these libraries are installed, you can import and use them in your script to perform natural language processing tasks such as tokenization, stemming, and lemmatization.

2

Chapter 2: Utilizing Conditional Statements

ChatGPT is a powerful language model that can generate a wide range of text, from simple responses to complex stories and articles. One way to get even more out of ChatGPT is to use conditional statements to control its output based on specific inputs. This chapter will show you how to use if-else statements to customize the behavior of ChatGPT and create more interactive and engaging chatbot applications.

Example: Let's say you want to create a simple chatbot that can answer questions about different types of animals. You can use an if-else statement to control the output of ChatGPT based on the user's input.

First, you'll need to define a list of keywords that will trigger different responses from ChatGPT. For example:

```python
if input == "dog":
    print("Dogs are a type of mammal and a common household pet.")

elif input == "cat":
    print("Cats are also a type of mammal and a popular pet.")

else:
    print("I'm sorry, I don't know much about that animal.")
```

Step 1: Create a new python file To start, open your preferred text editor or IDE and create a new python file. You can name it whatever you like, for example

chatbot.py.

Step 2: Define the keywords In this example, we're going to create a simple chatbot that can answer questions about different types of animals. So, you'll need to define a list of keywords that will trigger different responses from ChatGPT.

For example, you can define a list of keywords like this:

```python
keywords = ["dog", "cat", "bird", "fish", "snake"]
```

Step 3: Get the user input Now you'll need to get the user input. You can use the **input()** function to get the user input.

```python
input = input("What do you want to know about animal: ")
```

This line of code will prompt the user to enter an input and store it in the variable **input**.

Step 4: Use if-else statement Now that we have the user input, we can use the if-else statement to control the output of ChatGPT based on the user's input.

```python
if input in keywords:
    if input == "dog":
        print("Dogs are a type of mammal and a common household
        pet.")
    elif input == "cat":
        print("Cats are also a type of mammal and a popular pet.")
    elif input == "bird":
        print("Birds are warm-blooded feathered vertebrates.")
    elif input == "fish":
        print("Fish are cold-blooded aquatic animals.")
    elif input == "snake":
        print("Snakes are cold-blooded reptiles.")
else:
    print("I'm sorry, I don't know much about that animal.")
```

This code will check if the user input is in the keywords list and then check for each keyword and return the corresponding output. If the input is not in the keywords list, the code will return the default output.

Step 5: Run the script You can now save the script and run it in the command prompt or terminal by running he command **python chatbot.py**. The script will prompt the user to enter an input, and based on the input, it will return the corresponding output.

Step 6: Customize the output You can customize the output as per your requirement, for example, you can use the OpenAI API to generate more detailed and accurate responses for each keyword. Here is an example:

```python
import openai
openai.api_key = "YOUR_API_KEY"
if input in keywords:
    if input == "dog":
        response =
        openai.Completion.create(engine="text-davinci-002",
        prompt='Dogs are a type of mammal and a common household
        pet. Can you tell me more about dogs?')
        print(response["choices"][0]["text"])
    elif input == "cat":
        response =
        openai.Completion.create(engine="text-davinci-002",
        prompt='Cats are also a type of mammal and a popular pet.
        Can you tell me more about cats?')
        print(response["choices"][0]["text"])
```

This will use the OpenAI API to generate a more detailed and accurate response for each keyword.

Conclusion: With this approach, you can use conditional statements to control the output of ChatGPT based on specific inputs and create more interactive and engaging chatbot applications. This is just the tip of the iceberg, you can use this approach to create more complex applications like language translation, question answering, etc.

3

Chapter 3: Utilizing Variables and Loops

Introduction: In this chapter, we will learn how to use variables and loops to create more dynamic and powerful applications with ChatGPT. Variables allow us to store and manipulate data, while loops allow us to repeat certain actions multiple times. Together, they can be used to create a wide range of interactive and engaging chatbot applications.

Example: Let's say we want to create a chatbot that can generate a list of random numbers. We can use a loop to generate a specific number of random numbers and store them in a variable.

Step 1: Import the random module To generate random numbers, we need to import the random module in python. You can do this by adding the following line at the top of your script:

```
import random
```

Step 2: Define the number of random numbers Next, we need to define the number of random numbers we want to generate. You can do this by creating a variable and assigning it a value. For example:

```
number_of_numbers = 5
```

Step 3: Create an empty list To store the random numbers, we need to create an empty list. You can do this by creating a variable and assigning it an empty list. For example:

```
random_numbers = []
```

Step 4: Use a loop to generate random numbers Now we can use a for loop to generate the specified number of random numbers. We will use the **randint()** function from the random module to generate a random number between 1 and 100, and append it to the 'random_numberslist'. The loop should look like this:

```
for i in range(number_of_numbers):
    random_numbers.append(random.randint(1, 100))
```

This loop will run **number_of_numbers** times, and in each iteration, it will generate a random number between 1 and 100 and append it to the **random_numbers** list.

Step 5: Print the random numbers Finally, we can use the **print()** function to display the random numbers. You can do this by calling the **random_numbers** variable. For example:

```
print(random_numbers)
```

Here is an example of all the code from this chapter:

```
import random

# Define the number of random numbers
number_of_numbers = 5

# Create an empty list to store the random numbers
random_numbers = []
```

```python
# Use a loop to generate random numbers
for i in range(number_of_numbers):
    random_numbers.append(random.randint(1, 100))

# Print the random numbers
print(random_numbers)
```

Step 6: Run the script You can now save the script and run it in the command prompt or terminal by running the command **python chatbot.py**. The script will generate the specified number of random numbers and print them to the screen.

Conclusion: In this chapter, we've learned how to use variables and loops to create more dynamic and powerful applications with ChatGPT. By using variables, we can store and manipulate data, while loops allow us to repeat certain actions multiple times. With these tools, you can create a wide range of interactive and engaging chatbot applications.

4

Chapter 4: Utilizing Functions

In this chapter, we will learn how to use functions to create more organized and reusable code with ChatGPT. Functions allow us to group together a set of related code and call it multiple times with different arguments. This can make our code more readable, maintainable and reusable.

Example: Let's say we want to create a chatbot that can tell the weather in different cities. We can use a function to get the weather information from the OpenAI API and call it multiple times with different city names as an argument.

Step 1: Import the OpenAI library To use the OpenAI API, we need to import the openai library. You can do this by adding the following line at the top of your script:

```
import openai
```

Step 2: Define the function Next, we need to define a function that will take a city name as an argument and return the weather information. You can do this by creating a function and defining the arguments and the code that will be executed. For example:

```
def get_weather(city):
    openai.api_key = "YOUR_API_KEY"
```

```python
    response = openai.Completion.create(engine="text-davinci-002",
    prompt=f'What is the weather like in {city}?')
    return response["choices"][0]["text"]
```

Step 3: Call the function Now that we have defined the function, we can call it multiple times with different city names as an argument. For example:

```python
city_name = input("Enter the city name: ")
print(get_weather(city_name))
```

This code will prompt the user to enter a city name, and then it will call the **get_weather()** function with the entered city name as an argument and print the weather information returned by the function.

Step 4: Run the script

```python
import openai

def get_weather(city):
    openai.api_key = "YOUR_API_KEY"
    response = openai.Completion.create(engine="text-davinci-002",
    prompt=f'What is the weather like in {city}?')
    return response["choices"][0]["text"]

city_name = input("Enter the city name: ")
print(get_weather(city_name))
```

You can now save the script and run it in the command prompt or terminal by running the command **python chatbot.py**. The script will prompt the user to enter a city name and return the weather information of that city.

Conclusion: In this chapter, we've learned how to use functions to create more organized and reusable code with ChatGPT. By using functions, we can group together a set of related code and call it multiple times with different arguments. This can make our code more readable, maintainable and reusable.

5

Chapter 5: Using ChatGPT to Generate Text in Specific Styles or Formats

In this chapter, we will learn how to use ChatGPT to generate text in specific styles or formats, such as poetry or news articles. We can use the OpenAI API to fine-tune the model to generate text in specific styles and formats by providing it with examples of the desired style or format.

Example: Let's say we want to use ChatGPT to generate poetry. We can use the OpenAI API to fine-tune the model on a dataset of poems and then use the fine-tuned model to generate new poems.

Step 1: Gather a dataset of examples The first step is to gather a dataset of examples of the desired style or format. In this case, we need a dataset of poems. You can find such datasets online, for example, on Kaggle.

Step 2: Fine-tune the model Next, we need to fine-tune the model on the dataset of examples. You can do this by using the OpenAI API to train the model on the dataset. For example:

```python
import openai
openai.api_key = "YOUR_API_KEY"
model_engine = "text-davinci-002"
prompt = (f"Train a {model_engine} model on a dataset of poems")
response = openai.Ensemble.create(
```

```python
    prompt=prompt,
    dataset="dataset-of-poems",
    temperature=0.5,
    max_tokens=2048,
)
```

This code will use the **dataset-of-poems** to fine-tune the model, and you will get the id of the fine-tuned model, use this id to generate text.

Step 3: Use the fine-tuned model to generate text Once the model is fine-tuned, you can use it to generate new poems by providing it with a prompt. For example:

```python
prompt = (f"Write a poem about nature")
response = openai.Completion.create(engine=response["id"],
prompt=prompt)
print(response["choices"][0]["text"])
```

This code will use the fine-tuned model to generate a poem about nature.

Step 4: Run the script:

```python
import openai
openai.api_key = "YOUR_API_KEY"
model_engine = "text-davinci-002"

# Fine-tune the model
prompt = (f"Train a {model_engine} model on a dataset of poems")
response = openai.Ensemble.create(
    prompt=prompt,
    dataset="dataset-of-poems",
    temperature=0.5,
    max_tokens=2048,
)

# Use the fine-tuned model to generate text
prompt = (f"Write a poem about nature")
response = openai.Completion.create(engine=response["id"],
```

```
    prompt=prompt)
print(response["choices"][0]["text"])
```

You can now save the script and run it in the command prompt or terminal by running the command **python chatbot.py**. The script will fine-tune the model and generate a poem about nature.

Conclusion: In this chapter, we've learned how to use ChatGPT to generate text in specific styles or formats, such as poetry or news articles. By fine-tuning the model on a dataset of examples, we can generate text that is in the desired style or format.

6

Chapter 6: Advanced Techniques for Generating Text in Specific Styles or Formats

Introduction: In this chapter, we will learn some more advanced techniques for using ChatGPT to generate text in specific styles or formats, such as poetry or news articles. We will explore how to use different parameters and settings to fine-tune the model for specific styles or formats, and how to use multiple models to generate text.

Example: Let's say we want to use ChatGPT to generate poetry in different styles and formats. We can use the OpenAI API to fine-tune the model on different datasets of poems and use the fine-tuned models to generate new poems in the desired style or format.

Step 1: Gather multiple datasets of examples The first step is to gather multiple datasets of examples of different styles or formats of poetry. You can find such datasets online, for example, on Kaggle.

Step 2: Fine-tune the model on different datasets Next, we need to fine-tune the model on different datasets of examples. You can do this by using the OpenAI API to train the model on different datasets. For example:

```python
import openai
openai.api_key = "YOUR_API_KEY"
model_engine = "text-davinci-002"

# Fine-tune the model on a dataset of Haiku poems
prompt = (f"Train a {model_engine} model on a dataset of Haiku
poems")
response_haiku = openai.Ensemble.create(
prompt=prompt,
dataset="dataset-of-haiku-poems",
temperature=0.5,
max_tokens=2048,
)

Fine-tune the model on a dataset of Sonnet poems
prompt = (f"Train a {model_engine} model on a dataset of Sonnet
poems")
response_sonnet = openai.Ensemble.create(
prompt=prompt,
dataset="dataset-of-sonnet-poems",
temperature=0.5,
max_tokens=2048,
)
```

This code will fine-tune two models on different datasets, one for Haiku poems and one for Sonnet poems. You will get the id of each fine-tuned model and use them to generate text.

Step 3: Use the fine-tuned models to generate text Once the models are fine-tuned, you can use them to generate new poems in the desired style or format by providing them with a prompt. For example:

```python
prompt = input("Enter a prompt for the poem: ")
response_haiku =
openai.Completion.create(engine=response_haiku["id"],
prompt=prompt)
response_sonnet =
```

```python
openai.Completion.create(engine=response_sonnet["id"],
prompt=prompt)

print("Haiku Poem:")
print(response_haiku["choices"][0]["text"])
print("Sonnet Poem:")
print(response_sonnet["choices"][0]["text"])
```

This code will prompt the user to enter a prompt for the poem, and then use the fine-tuned models to generate a Haiku poem and a Sonnet poem based on the prompt. It will then print both the poems.

Step 4: Experiment with different parameters and settings To fine-tune the model for specific styles or formats, you can experiment with different parameters and settings. For example, you can try different temperatures, max tokens, and prompt lengths. You can also try different models and engines to see which one generates text that best fits your desired style or format.

Step 5: Run the script You can now save the script and run it in the command prompt or terminal by running the command 'python chatbot.py'. The script will fine-tune the model and generate a Haiku poem and a Sonnet poem based on the user's prompt.

Conclusion: In this chapter, we've learned some more advanced techniques for using ChatGPT to generate text in specific styles or formats, such as poetry or news articles. By fine-tuning the model on different datasets and experimenting with different parameters and settings, we can generate text that is in the desired style or format.

7

Chapter 7: Using ChatGPT to Generate Code or Other Structured Output

In this chapter, we will learn how to use ChatGPT to generate code or other structured output. We can use the OpenAI API to fine-tune the model to generate code or other structured output by providing it with examples of the desired output.

Example: Let's say we want to use ChatGPT to generate Python code to calculate the factorial of a number. We can use the OpenAI API to fine-tune the model on a dataset of Python code and use the fine-tuned model to generate new code to calculate the factorial of a number.

Step 1: Gather a dataset of examples The first step is to gather a dataset of examples of the desired output. In this case, we need a dataset of Python code to calculate the factorial of a number. You can find such datasets online, for example, on Github.

Step 2: Fine-tune the model Next, we need to fine-tune the model on the dataset of examples. You can do this by using the OpenAI API to train the model on the dataset. For example:

```
import openai
openai.api_key = "YOUR_API_KEY"
```

```python
model_engine = "text-davinci-002"
prompt = (f"Train a {model_engine} model on a dataset of Python
code to calculate the factorial of a number")
response = openai.Ensemble.create(
    prompt=prompt,
    dataset="dataset-of-Python-code-factorial",
    temperature=0.5,
    max_tokens=2048,
)
```

This code will use the **dataset-of-Python-code-factorial** to fine-tune the model, and you will get the id of the fine-tuned model, use this id to generate text.

Step 3: Use the fine-tuned model to generate code Once the model is fine-tuned, you can use it to generate new code to calculate the factorial of a number by providing it with a prompt. For example:

```python
prompt = (f"Write a Python code to calculate the factorial of a
number")
response = openai.Completion.create(engine=response["id"],
prompt=prompt)
print(response["choices"][0]["text"])
```

This code will use the fine-tuned model to generate a Python code to calculate the factorial of a number.

Step 4: Run the script You can now save the script and run it in the command prompt or terminal by running the command **python chatbot.py**. The script will fine-tune the model and generate a Python code to calculate the factorial of a number.

Conclusion: In this chapter, we've learned how to use ChatGPT to generate code or other structured output. By fine-tuning the model on a dataset of examples, we can generate code or other structured output that is in the desired format.

8

Chapter 8: Utilizing ChatGPT for Language Translation or Text Summarization

In this chapter, we will learn how to use ChatGPT to generate language translations or text summaries. We can use the OpenAI API to fine-tune the model on a dataset of language translations or text summaries and use the fine-tuned model to generate new translations or summaries.

Example: Let's say we want to use ChatGPT to generate a summary of a given text. We can use the OpenAI API to fine-tune the model on a dataset of text summaries and use the fine-tuned model to generate a summary of a given text.

Step 1: Gather a dataset of examples The first step is to gather a dataset of examples of the desired output. In this case, we need a dataset of text summaries. You can find such datasets online, for example, on Kaggle.

Step 2: Fine-tune the model Next, we need to fine-tune the model on the dataset of examples. You can do this by using the OpenAI API to train the model on the dataset. For example:

```
import openai
openai.api_key = "YOUR_API_KEY"
model_engine = "text-davinci-002"
prompt = (f"Train a {model_engine} model on a dataset of text
```

```
summaries")
response = openai.Ensemble.create(
    prompt=prompt,
    dataset="dataset-of-text-summaries",
    temperature=0.5,
    max_tokens=2048,
)
```

This code will use the **dataset-of-text-summaries** to fine-tune the model, and you will get the id of the fine-tuned model, use this id to generate text.

Step 3: Use the fine-tuned model to generate summary Once the model is fine-tuned, you can use it to generate a summary of a given text by providing it with a prompt. For example:

```
text = input("Enter the text you want to summarize: ")
prompt = (f"summarize this text: {text}")
response = openai.Completion.create(engine=response["id"],
prompt=prompt)
print(response["choices"][0]["text"])
```

This code will prompt the user to enter a text, and then use the fine-tuned model to generate a summary of the given text.

Step 4: Run the script You can now save the script and run it in the command prompt or terminal by running the command **python chatbot.py**. The script will fine-tune the model and generate a summary of the given text.

Conclusion: In this chapter, we've learned how to use ChatGPT to generate language translations or text summaries. By fine-tuning the model on a dataset of examples, we can generate translations or summaries that are in the desired format.

9

Chapter 9: Creating Prompts that Encourage ChatGPT to Generate Creative or Original Content

In this chapter, we will learn how to create prompts that encourage ChatGPT to generate creative or original content, such as writing stories or jokes. We can use different techniques such as using open-ended prompts, providing a starting point, or using specific prompts to generate creative or original content.

Example: Let's say we want to use ChatGPT to generate a creative story. We can use an open-ended prompt and provide a starting point to encourage the model to generate a creative story.

Step 1: Create an open-ended prompt The first step is to create an open-ended prompt that encourages the model to generate creative or original content. For example: "Write a story about a magical world where animals can talk"

Step 2: Provide a starting point Next, we need to provide a starting point for the model to generate the story. For example: "Once upon a time, in a magical forest, there lived a group of animals who could talk."

Step 3: Use specific prompts Additionally, we can use specific prompts to encourage the model to generate creative or original content. For example, we can ask the model to generate a surprise ending, or to include a specific character or plot twist in the story.

Step 4: Run the script You can now use the OpenAI API to generate the story by providing it with the prompt and the starting point, for example:

```python
import openai
openai.api_key = "YOUR_API_KEY"
prompt = "Write a story about a magical world where animals can
talk. Once upon a time, in a magical forest, there lived a group
of animals who could talk."
response = openai.Completion.create(engine="text-davinci-002",
prompt=prompt, temperature=0.5, max_tokens=2048)
print(response["choices"][0]["text"])
```

This code will use the prompt and the starting point to generate a story about a magical world where animals can talk.

Step 5: Experiment with different techniques To generate even more creative or original content, you can experiment with different techniques such as using different models or engines, adjusting the temperature, or using different max_tokens.

Conclusion: In this chapter, we've learned how to create prompts that encourage ChatGPT to generate creative or original content. By using open-ended prompts, providing a starting point, and using specific prompts, we can generate stories, jokes, and other creative content.

Chapter 10: Incorporating Domain-Specific Knowledge into Prompts

In this chapter, we will learn how to incorporate domain-specific knowledge, such as medical or legal terminology, into prompts to generate more accurate and specialized output. By fine-tuning the model on a dataset that contains domain-specific knowledge, we can generate output that is more accurate and relevant to the specific domain.

Example 1: Medical Domain Let's say we want to use ChatGPT to generate medical reports. We can use the OpenAI API to fine-tune the model on a dataset of medical reports and use the fine-tuned model to generate new medical reports.

Step 1: Gather a dataset of examples The first step is to gather a dataset of examples of the desired output. In this case, we need a dataset of medical reports. You can find such datasets online, for example, on OpenHealthData.

Step 2: Fine-tune the model Next, we need to fine-tune the model on the dataset of examples. You can do this by using the OpenAI API to train the model on the dataset. For example:

```
import openai
openai.api_key = "YOUR_API_KEY"
```

```
model_engine = "text-davinci-002"
prompt = (f"Train a {model_engine} model on a dataset of medical
reports")
response = openai.Ensemble.create(
    prompt=prompt,
    dataset="dataset-of-medical-reports",
    temperature=0.5,
    max_tokens=2048,
)
```

This code will use the **dataset-of-medical-reports** to fine-tune the model, and you will get the id of the fine-tuned model, use this id to generate text.

Step 3: Use the fine-tuned model to generate medical reports Once the model is fine-tuned, you can use it to generate medical reports by providing it with a prompt. For example:

```
patient_data = input("Enter the patient data: ")
prompt = (f"Generate a medical report for a patient with the
following information: {patient_data}")
response = openai.Completion.create(engine=response["id"],
prompt=prompt)
print(response["choices"][0]["text"])
```

This code will prompt the user to enter patient data, and then use the fine-tuned model to generate a medical report based on that information.

Example 2: Legal Domain Let's say we want to use ChatGPT to generate legal documents. We can use the OpenAI API to fine-tune the model on a dataset of legal documents and use the fine-tuned model to generate new legal documents.

Step 1: Gather a dataset of examples The first step is to gather a dataset of examples of the desired output. In this case, we need a dataset of legal documents. You can find such datasets online, for example, on LawDataset.

Step 2: Fine-tune the model Next, we need to fine-tune the model on the dataset of examples. You can do this by using the OpenAI API to train the model on the dataset. For example:

```python
import openai
openai.api_key = "YOUR_API_KEY"
model_engine = "text-davinci-002"
prompt = (f"Train a {model_engine} model on a dataset of legal
documents")
response = openai.Ensemble.create(
    prompt=prompt,
    dataset="dataset-of-legal-documents",
    temperature=0.5,
    max_tokens=2048,
)
```

This code will use the **dataset-of-legal-documents** to fine-tune the model, and you will get the id of the fine-tuned model, use this id to generate text.

Step 3: Use the fine-tuned model to generate legal documents Once the model is fine-tuned, you can use it to generate legal documents by providing it with a prompt. For example:

```python
case_data = input("Enter the case data: ")
prompt = (f"Generate a legal document for a case with the
following information: {case_data}")
response = openai.Completion.create(engine=response["id"],
prompt=prompt)
print(response["choices"][0]["text"])
```

This code will prompt the user to enter case data, and then use the fine-tuned model to generate a legal document based on that information.

Conclusion: In this chapter, we've learned how to incorporate domain-specific knowledge into prompts to generate more accurate and specialized output. By fine-tuning the model on a dataset of examples from a specific domain, we can generate output that is more accurate and relevant to that domain. The examples shown here are for medical and legal domain, but the same process can be used for any other domain by fine-tuning the model on a dataset from that domain.

11

Chapter 11: Using ChatGPT to Complete Tasks

In this chapter, we will learn how to use ChatGPT to complete tasks such as answering questions, solving problems, or providing explanations. We can use the OpenAI API to generate output that is specific to a given task and use it to complete the task.

Example 1: Answering Questions Let's say we want to use ChatGPT to answer questions. We can use the OpenAI API to generate an answer to a given question by providing it with a prompt.

Step 1: Create a prompt The first step is to create a prompt that contains the question. For example: "What is the capital of France?"

Step 2: Use the OpenAI API to generate an answer Next, we need to use the OpenAI API to generate an answer to the question by providing it with the prompt. For example:

```python
import openai
openai.api_key = "YOUR_API_KEY"
prompt = "What is the capital of France?"
response = openai.Completion.create(engine="text-davinci-002",
prompt=prompt)
print(response["choices"][0]["text"])
```

This code will use the prompt to generate an answer to the question: "What is the capital of France?"

Step 3: Use the generated output Once we have the answer, we can use it to complete the task of answering the question.

Example 2: Solving Problems Let's say we want to use ChatGPT to solve a mathematical problem. We can use the OpenAI API to generate the solution to a given problem by providing it with a prompt.

Step 1: Create a prompt The first step is to create a prompt that contains the problem. For example: "Solve the equation 2x + 3 = 7"

Step 2: Use the OpenAI API to generate a solution Next, we need to use the OpenAI API to generate a solution to the problem by providing it with the prompt. For example:

```
import openai
openai.api_key = "YOUR_API_KEY"
prompt = "Solve the equation 2x + 3 = 7"
response = openai.Completion.create(engine="text-davinci-002",
prompt=prompt)
print(response["choices"][0]["text"])
```

This code will use the prompt to generate a solution to the problem: "Solve the equation 2x + 3 = 7"

Step 3: Use the generated output Once we have the solution, we can use it to complete the task of solving the problem.

Example 3: Providing explanations Let's say we want to use ChatGPT to provide explanations for a given topic. We can use the OpenAI API to generate an explanation for a given topic by providing it with a prompt.

Step 1: Create a prompt The first step is to create a prompt that contains the topic. For example: "Explain how a car engine works"

Step 2: Use the OpenAI API to generate an explanation Next, we need to use the OpenAI API to generate an explanation for the topic by providing it with the prompt. For example:

```python
import openai
openai.api_key = "YOUR_API_KEY"
prompt = "Explain how a car engine works"
response = openai.Completion.create(engine="text-davinci-002",
prompt=prompt)
print(response["choices"][0]["text"])
```

This code will use the prompt to generate an explanation for the topic: "Explain how a car engine works"

Step 3: Use the generated output Once we have the explanation, we can use it to complete the task of providing an explanation for the given topic.

Conclusion: In this chapter, we've learned how to use ChatGPT to complete tasks such as answering questions, solving problems, and providing explanations. By providing ChatGPT with a prompt specific to a given task, we can generate output that can be used to complete that task. This can be used in a variety of applications, such as creating a virtual assistant or an AI-powered tutoring system.

12

Chapter 12: Using ChatGPT to Generate Text with Specific Emotions

In this chapter, we will learn how to use ChatGPT to generate text with specific emotions, such as sad or happy. We can use the OpenAI API to fine-tune the model on a dataset of text labeled with specific emotions and use the fine-tuned model to generate new text with those emotions.

Example 1: Generating sad text Let's say we want to use ChatGPT to generate sad text. We can use the OpenAI API to fine-tune the model on a dataset of sad text and use the fine-tuned model to generate new sad text.

Step 1: Gather a dataset of sad examples The first step is to gather a dataset of examples of sad text. You can find such datasets online, for example, on Sentiment140 dataset.

Step 2: Fine-tune the model Next, we need to fine-tune the model on the dataset of sad examples. You can do this by using the OpenAI API to train the model on the dataset. For example:

```
import openai
openai.api_key = "YOUR_API_KEY"
model_engine = "text-davinci-002"
prompt = (f"Train a {model_engine} model on a dataset of sad text")
response = openai.Ensemble.create(
```

```
    prompt=prompt,
    dataset="dataset-of-sad-text",
    temperature=0.5,
    max_tokens=2048,
)
```

This code will use the **dataset-of-sad-text** to fine-tune the model, and you will get the id of the fine-tuned model, use this id to generate text.

Step 3: Use the fine-tuned model to generate sad text Once the model is fine-tuned, you can use it to generate sad text by providing it with a prompt. For example:

```
prompt = "Generate a sad story"
response = openai.Completion.create(engine=response["id"],
prompt=prompt)
print(response["choices"][0]["text"])
```

This code will use the fine-tuned model to generate a sad story based on the prompt

Example 2: Generating happy text We can use the same process to generate happy text. We just need to gather a dataset of examples of happy text and fine-tune the model on that dataset.

Step 1: Gather a dataset of happy examples The first step is to gather a dataset of examples of happy text. You can find such datasets online, for example, on Sentiment140 dataset.

Step 2: Fine-tune the model Next, we need to fine-tune the model on the dataset of happy examples. You can do this by using the OpenAI API to train the model on the dataset. For example:

```
import openai
openai.api_key = "YOUR_API_KEY"
model_engine = "text-davinci-002"
prompt = (f"Train a {model_engine} model on a dataset of happy
text")
```

```
response = openai.Ensemble.create(
    prompt=prompt,
    dataset="dataset-of-happy-text",
    temperature=0.5,
    max_tokens=2048,
)
```

This code will use the **dataset-of-happy-text** to fine-tune the model, and you will get the id of the fine-tuned model, use this id to generate text.

Step 3: Use the fine-tuned model to generate happy text Once the model is fine-tuned, you can use it to generate happy text by providing it with a prompt. For example:

```
prompt = "Generate a happy story"
response = openai.Completion.create(engine=response["id"],
prompt=prompt)
print(response["choices"][0]["text"])
```

This code will use the fine-tuned model to generate a happy story based on the prompt.

Conclusion: In this chapter, we've learned how to use ChatGPT to generate text with specific emotions, such as sad or happy. By fine-tuning the model on a dataset of text labeled with specific emotions, we can use the fine-tuned model to generate new text with those emotions. This can be used in a variety of applications, such as creating an AI-powered emotional chatbot or a sentiment analysis tool.

It's worth mentioning that fine-tuning a model for specific emotions can be a time-consuming process that requires a large dataset, but it can also be very powerful if done correctly. You can also experiment with fine-tuning the model on different emotions and different datasets of text to achieve better results.

13

Chapter 13: Combining ChatGPT with Other AI Models or Tools

In this chapter, we will learn how to combine ChatGPT with other AI models or tools to create more powerful and versatile applications. By combining the capabilities of different AI models or tools, we can create applications that can perform more advanced tasks and produce more accurate results.

Example 1: Combining ChatGPT with a Named Entity Recognition (NER) model Let's say we want to use ChatGPT to generate text that includes specific named entities, such as people, locations, or organizations. We can use a Named Entity Recognition (NER) model to extract named entities from text and provide them to ChatGPT as input.

Step 1: Use a NER model to extract named entities The first step is to use a NER model, such as SpaCy, to extract named entities from text. For example:

```
import spacy

# Load the spacy model
nlp = spacy.load("en_core_web_sm")

# Process the text
doc = nlp("Barack Obama was born in Honolulu, Hawaii.")
```

```python
# Extract the named entities
named_entities = [ent.text for ent in doc.ents]
print(named_entities)
```

This code will extract the named entities "Barack Obama" and "Honolulu, Hawaii" from the text.

Step 2: Provide the named entities to ChatGPT Next, we need to provide the named entities to ChatGPT as input and use them to generate text. For example:

```python
import openai
openai.api_key = "YOUR_API_KEY"
prompt = "Generate text about {} and {}".format(named_entities[0],
named_entities[1])
response = openai.Completion.create(engine="text-davinci-002",
prompt=prompt)
print(response["choices"][0]["text"])
```

This code will use the named entities extracted from the previous step to generate text that includes them.

Example 2: Combining ChatGPT with a Text-to-Speech (TTS) model Let's say we want to use ChatGPT to generate text that can be spoken out by a computer. We can use a Text-to-Speech (TTS) model to convert the text generated by ChatGPT into speech.

Step 1: Use ChatGPT to generate text The first step is to use ChatGPT to generate text as we've done in previous examples.

Step 2: Use a TTS model to convert text to speech Next, we need to use a TTS model, such as Google's Cloud TTS API, to convert the text generated by ChatGPT into speech. For example:

```python
from google.cloud import texttospeech

# Instantiates a client
client = texttospeech.TextToSpeechClient()
```

```python
# Set the text input to be synthesized
synthesis_input =
texttospeech.types.SynthesisInput(text=response["choices"][0]["text"])


# Build the voice request, select the language code ("en-US") and
the ssml
# voice gender ("neutral")
voice = texttospeech.types.VoiceSelectionParams(
    language_code="en-US",
    ssml_gender=texttospeech.enums.SsmlVoiceGender.NEUTRAL)


# Select the type of audio file you want returned
audio_config = texttospeech.types.AudioConfig(
    audio_encoding=texttospeech.enums.AudioEncoding.MP3)


# Perform the text-to-speech request on the text input with the
selected
# voice parameters and audio file type
response = client.synthesize_speech(synthesis_input, voice,
audio_config)


# The response's audio_content is binary.
with open("output.mp3", "wb") as out:
    out.write(response.audio_content)
    print("Audio content written to file 'output.mp3'")
```

This code will use the text generated by ChatGPT and convert it into speech using the Google Cloud TTS API.

Conclusion: In this chapter, we've learned how to combine ChatGPT with other AI models or tools to create more powerful and versatile applications. By using NER models, TTS models or other AI models and tools in conjunction with ChatGPT, we can create applications that can perform more advanced tasks and produce more accurate results. This can be used in a variety of applications, such as creating an AI-powered language translator, a question answering system, or a chatbot.

14

Chapter 14: Ethical Considerations when working with GPT-like models

In this chapter, we will learn about the ethical considerations when working with GPT-like models. GPT-like models, such as GPT-2 and GPT-3, are powerful tools that can generate human-like text, but they also have the potential to perpetuate biases and misinformation. As such, it is important to be aware of the ethical implications of using these models and to take steps to mitigate any potential harms.

Bias in GPT-like models: GPT-like models are trained on large amounts of text data, which means that they may inadvertently learn biases from the data. For example, if a model is trained on a dataset that contains a disproportionate amount of text written by men, it may generate text that is more likely to use male pronouns or to describe men in positions of power. Similarly, if a model is trained on a dataset that contains a lot of text that is racist or sexist, it may generate text that perpetuates those biases.

Mitigating bias: There are several ways to mitigate bias in GPT-like models. One approach is to fine-tune the model on a more diverse dataset, which can help to correct for any biases that the model may have learned from the original training data. Another approach is to use techniques such as bias-correction or de-biasing, which can help to reduce the amount of bias in the generated text.

Another way to mitigate bias is by using techniques like counterfactual data augmentation or adversarial training, these methods can be used to make the model more robust to biased inputs.

Transparency and accountability: When working with GPT-like models, it is important to be transparent about the model's capabilities and limitations. This includes being clear about the model's training data, how it was trained, and what types of text it is capable of generating. Additionally, it's important to be accountable for the output of the model, and to be prepared to take action if the model generates text that is harmful or offensive.

Conclusion: In this chapter, we've learned about the ethical considerations when working with GPT-like models, such as GPT-2 and GPT-3. We've discussed the potential for these models to perpetuate biases and misinformation, and have explored ways to mitigate these risks, such as fine-tuning the model on a more diverse dataset, using bias-correction or de-biasing techniques, and being transparent and accountable for the model's output. As AI developers and researchers, it's important to consider the ethical implications of our work and to take steps to mitigate any potential harms.

15

Chapter 15: Conclusion

In this book, we've explored a wide range of techniques for utilizing ChatGPT, an advanced language model developed by OpenAI. We've learned how to fine-tune the model on custom data, how to use conditional statements to control the output of the model, how to generate text in specific styles or formats, how to generate code or other structured output, and how to incorporate domain-specific knowledge. We also covered ethical considerations and ways to combine ChatGPT with other AI models or tools to create more powerful and versatile applications.

Key takeaways:

- ChatGPT is a powerful language model that can be fine-tuned to generate text in a wide range of styles and formats.
- Conditional statements can be used to control the output of the model based on specific inputs.
- Advanced techniques like fine-tuning, conditioning, and generating specific types of text can be applied to GPT-3, but it also requires more computational resources and the use of the OpenAI API.
- It's important to be aware of the ethical implications of using GPT-like models and to take steps to mitigate any potential harms.

Additional resources:

- OpenAI's website (**https://openai.com/**) – The official website of OpenAI, which provides documentation, tutorials, and resources for working with ChatGPT and other AI models.
- GitHub (**https://github.com/**) – A platform for sharing and collaborating on code, which has a wealth of resources and examples for working with ChatGPT and other AI models.
- AI Ethics Lab (**https://ai-ethics-lab.org/**) – A resource for information and guidance on the ethical implications of AI and machine learning.

FAQ: Q: How can I fine-tune ChatGPT on my own data? A: You can fine-tune ChatGPT on your own data by providing the model with a dataset of text that is relevant to your use case. This can be done by using the OpenAI API to train the model on your dataset, or by using the Hugging Face's transformers library to fine-tune the model locally.

Q: How can I use ChatGPT to generate code? A: ChatGPT can be used to generate code by providing it with a prompt that describes the desired code output and fine-tuning the model on a dataset of code examples. Additionally, you can use techniques like beam search or sampling to increase the likelihood of the model generating valid code.

Q: How can I ensure that ChatGPT's output is not biased? A: To ensure that ChatGPT's output is not biased, you can fine-tune the model on a more diverse dataset and use techniques like bias-correction or de-biasing. Additionally, you can use techniques like counterfactual data augmentation or adversarial training to make the model more robust to biased inputs.

Q: What are the limitations of ChatGPT? A: ChatGPT is a powerful model, but it has limitations. It can generate human-like text, but it is not capable of understanding the meaning of the text it generates. Additionally, it is limited by the quality and diversity of the data it was trained on, so it may inadvertently learn biases from the training data.

I hope this information is helpful and that this book has been informative and useful for you.

Cheers,

AI Mastery Solutions

40